About the author

Bishop Dr. David Oronsaye is a prophet to the Nations, a seasoned preacher with a mandate to stir up the body of Christ for the end time move of God. He functions powerfully in the prophetic, with signs and wonders following.

A true evangelist driven with a strong passion for the lost, he is also an author of several inspirational books.

He is the co-founder and general overseer of the All Nations Christian Centre international headquarters in London, England.

He is married to Rev. Judith Oronsaye and they are blessed with four daughters.

All Nations Christian Centre
15 York Hill, West Norwood,
London, SE27 0BU
E-mail: drdavid.ancc@gmail.com
Tel: +44 (0)20 8670 0300

Website: www.anccministries.org

Dedication

I dedicate this book to my
Inspirer,
Leader
and Teacher:
the Holy Spirit.

A leader must be able to make excellent decisions that respect and represent the values and interest of God.

THE POWER OF DECISION

Bishop Dr. David Oronsaye

Published in the United Kingdom by
Filament Publishing Ltd
16 Croydon Road, Waddon, Croydon,
Surrey, CR0 4PA, United Kingdom
+44(0)20 8688 2598
www.filamentpublishing.com

© 2015 Bishop Dr. David Oronsaye

ISBN 978-1-910819-33-3

Printed by IngramSpark

The right of Bishop Dr. David Oronsaye to be identified as the author of this work has been asserted by him in accordance with the Designs and Copyright Act 1988.

This book is subject to international copyright and may not be copied in any way without the prior written permission of the publishers.

Table of Contents

Introduction		9
Chapter One	Decision	11
Chapter Two	Impact of Decisions	21
Chapter Three	Vision and Visibility	35
Chapter Four	Wisdom Keys	56
Conclusion		69

The apostle Paul made a decision to serve God and follow him to the end, even unto death. Every decision we make in life determines and reveals what we stand for as well as the nature that we carry.

INTRODUCTION

Life is all about decision-making. Every day, we face different situations where we have to make choices based on our assessments of the issues. These choices may be in little and simple things such as what to eat and what to wear, or heavier matters like what business to invest in, how much to invest, who to marry, the best staff to recruit, and many more, as your case may be.

You are the way you are right now and exactly where you are now because of the choices you made yesterday. Your next level and location in life will also be determined by the decisions you will make today. A life without decision is divided, as decision is a powerful force that gives you decisive direction. Life without decision-making has got no future. Why? Simply because it would have lost its present and the present initiates the future. A man who lacks the decision-making ability is like a man who has lost the use of his two legs and is also blinded to the realities of life, therefore will not be able to move.

To stand well and to see well with a clear focus towards achieving good purpose in life, you must have good decision-making skills. Without it, life becomes a failure, an object of shame and disgrace. Having and also using the ability to make decisions is a sign of effective leadership and vice visa.

This book has looked at decision-making and how every decision you make can affect you and others, either positively or negatively and whether today or in the future. Every Christian should base their decisions on the principles of the word of God and the spirit of God. This book will make you more conscious of the realities of decision-making. Finally, it encourages you to connect with vital wisdom keys which, when imbibed, will cause you to make wise choices.

> The Holy Spirit is the master strategist and if you will allow him, he will guide you and you will find yourself always making the right decisions.

Chapter One

Decision

A leader must be able to make excellent decisions that respect and represent the values and interest of God. High level leadership needs high level results without compromise and indecision. A leader who does not have decision-making skills will find it hard to make progress. There are different levels of decision; good level is a catalyst in progress, speed and advancement with the power of upgrade. It can convert the failure of any individual, group or organisation to success. It has the lifting power from the valley to the mountain top.

It takes the help of God to make decisions that can upgrade above the hills. This means, above the will of man. His perfect will shall be exalted above the will of man, and many shall come to buy into the perfect will of God, and it takes good decision to do that.

Isaiah 2: 1- 3: "In the last days, the mountain of the Lord' house will be the highest of all very important places on earth. It will be raised above the other hills and people from all over the world will stream there to worship. People from many nations will come and say, come, let us go up to the mountain of the Lord, to the house of Jacob's God. There he will teach us his ways and we will walk in his paths"

Our lives are governed by the choices we make. Hasty decision-making when you are not well rested and are in a moment of frustration and discouragement in certain situations, will initiate bad result.

Decision must pass through God in the absence of 'yourself'. There is no need to make your own decisions before asking God for his opinion, because that will indicate that you only want God to confirm your own decision.

Good decision will not only produce result for the present, but also for posterity. The impact of a good decision goes from one generation to another. For example, Esther was a Jew who made up her mind to stand for what she believed (God's word) and notice that she fasted before presenting herself to the king. This means that she backed up her decision with prayers. Today, many years after she made that choice, we still read about her. In fact, we use her as a reference point for a number of different reasons: her ability to make a wise decision, her determination to stand by such decision, her boldness to go before the king without invitation. Mind you, it was extremely unacceptable to present oneself before the king without invitation at the time; the penalty could result in death sentence if the king was in a bad or unfavourable mood. Esther's faith to expect the best in the face of strong opposition and indeed death is a reference point today.

It will only take us to make a decision to come out from ourselves and serve God in order to obtain victory in every area of our lives. Decision-making has elements of risks; however, risk-taking should be done wisely and also, right decision prevents us from foolishness. Once the facts are clear, the decision practically jumps at you! Decisions should be made objectively, based on facts and not on assumptions.

The apostle Paul made a decision to serve God and follow him to the end, even unto death. Every decision we make in life determines and reveals what we stand for as well as the nature that we carry. Our decisions also reveal how engaged we are with the things of the one we portray and belong to. As a house built on rock is solid and can stand against the tests of time, so are our lives built by decisions and each one of the decisions we make adds up as collective destiny. If the decision is the right one based on the word of God, tendency is that it will stand the test of time because the word of God is like the solid rock. Successful people tend to make decisions very consciously and hardly change them, whilst unsuccessful people tend to make decisions that they change often and easily. Indecision is often the lack of energy. You have the power and the privilege of choice. A good leader ought to know that there are certain easy steps to follow in order to make the good decisions.

For example, clarify the issue; where am I? What do I need to do? Where do I want to be? What is the decision that I need to take to get me the results I want?

Gather your facts; some of the frequent mistakes made in decision-making include trying to decide before all the facts are known. Do not rely on assumptions, which means you should learn to question your assumptions and get the facts correct. Refuse to be put under any form of pressure into making decisions. Often, there are times where you may need to make a quick decision, especially if you are working with or in a group and, your team will want direction 'now': 'Let's get it settled now!' At such times, you may be compelled to make decisions too quickly. However, once you have clear facts, the right decision to make becomes very easy to see.

Get good counsel; you may need to get some advice; spiritual advice, financial advice or legal advice, as the case may be. A leader is a person of action and to be a person of action, you must master the act of decision-making, grow in maturity as well as be responsibly decisive. Successful leaders have the courage to take action where others hesitate. Your decision will always be better if you do what is right for others and not necessarily what is right by you. When working in a group, even though the input of other team members should be utilised, the final decision-making burden belongs to the leader. You cannot please everyone with your decisions, neither should you try to, but you have to be sure that you do the right thing. Bear in mind that decision-making may include some elements of risk-taking. You need to ask yourself, 'What are the risks involved?' because the level of risks would also impact on the choices you make.

You may also want to consider the following as they could be active forces behind making effective decisions.

The Place of Prayer in Decision-Making

Take your decision-making process in prayer before your maker, God almighty, without having made up your mind. That way, your own reasoning will not overshadow the voice of God. You really cannot genuinely want a decision from God knowing full well that you have made up your mind about the issue. Making your decision before asking for counsel is nonsense and does not show sincerity. When Jesus Christ was on earth, he never made decisions without the Father. For example, in John 5:20 he said of himself: *I do what I see my father do.*

Prayer is the key access in communicating with God for effective and efficient decision-making. It is a fellowship that gives you the privilege of knowing the mind of God concerning specific things. Every wise son seeks God's counsel before engaging in anything; be it marriage, business, education, relationship, whatever it may be. Well-balanced decisions will carry two things: joy and excellent testimony, whereas poor and bad decisions will cause pain and sorrow. This will not be your portion in Jesus' name!

The Holy Spirit in decision making

The super package for delivering desirable results in decision-making is by the agency of the Holy Spirit. When you let the Holy Spirit guide you in your decision-making, you will never get it wrong because he is the one that understands the past, he is in the present and he knows the future. He is not partial, neither is he double-minded and he will help you make decisions, according to the perfect will of God. Romans 8:26-28 says: *likewise the spirit also helps our infirmities: for we know not what we should pray for as we ought: but the Spirit himself makes intercessions for us with groaning which cannot be uttered.* The Holy Spirit is most reliable in excellent decision making.

In John 14: 26, Jesus said to his disciples, *but the comforter, which is the holy ghost, whom the father will send in my name, he shall teach you all things, and bring to your remembrance, whatsoever I have said unto you.* The Holy Spirit is the master strategist and if you will allow him, he will guide you and you will find yourself always making the right decisions.

God's Perspective

Decision-making should be in accordance with the way God sees things, avoiding human errors. It should be balanced on God's perfect will because God desires things to be done in order and in decency. Every decision taken in order and decency will initiate progress. A disorganised person is a product of disorganised decisions and thoughts. Decision should not be taken until you are organised. It is called organised decision to create a platform for actual execution of the decision you will make. A disorganised mind will make decisions that will lead to pitfalls and neglect.

Great atmosphere for sound judgement

When the atmosphere in which you are making your decision is intense, the sense of perfect judgement will be interrupted. Good sense of decision-making is a product of good atmosphere. Be sure of the environment where you are and if it is not conducive, go someplace else where your sense of good decision will not be blocked. Somewhere you can evaluate your facts and make a balanced decision. Let your mood be calm, quiet and calculated.

Be in a state of mental stability and calmness because confusion will interrupt your decision-making process. A mad person cannot make decisions for himself; talk more of making decision on behalf of a group. Why? It is because of mental instability.

If your mental state is unstable, you will likely make a nonsense and foolish decision. Why nonsense? Because there will be no sense in it! Why foolish? Because there will be no wisdom in it! Decision taken while your mental state of mind is unstable can pull down the roof and set a whole house on fire. Avoid making decisions until you are mentally stable and powerfully positioned in your mind. Your decision-making process can be reliable with outstanding clarity of thoughts. Because your sense is in your head, it is not acceptable by law of common sense to make decisions in time of crisis. You can make immediate decisions to come out of crisis but, you cannot make the kind of decision that will affect the destiny of others.

Foolish and unreasonable decisions are at many times the result of making decisions while in crisis. A depressed economist cannot make effective economic decisions for the country because he is depressed. He will only make depressive decisions that will destroy the country. It is therefore important to consider the mood that you are in when making decisions.

Balance your decisions with wisdom. Wisdom is the solution, the key principle of decision-making. Wisdom specialises in solving conflicts and puts balance on the decision-making process. When there is a promising and outstanding decision, behind it will be wisdom. When there is no wisdom, the people are disorganised. Get wisdom and organise your decision. A well-balanced decision has the heart of wisdom.

Evaluate your final decision with the eye of the word. Man may tell a lie but God and his word can be trusted. The word of God is true; it evaluates analyses and rearranges. Put it in the scale of the word of God and find out the result.

Do not announce your decision in a hasty mood. It must be properly evaluated. Decision has a governmental nature; it can cause revival or riot.

Decision should not be made based on the following: feelings and emotions, circumstances, subjective opinions, pride, anger, flesh, or third party subjective views.

The art of meditation

Meditation is a powerful force in decision-making. It brings understanding to every situation and gives perfect direction. Meditation on the word of God helps to release light to the journey of life. It helps to avoid unreasonable and hasty decisions that may cause more pain and multiple problems. In decision-making, the weapon of meditation is very effective and efficient in reaching good decision. Psalm 1: 1-3: *Blessed is the man that walketh not in the counsel of the ungodly, nor standeth in the way of sinners nor sitteth in the seat of the scornful but, his delight is in the law of the Lord and in his law doth he meditate day and night.*

He shall be like a tree planted by the rivers of water, that brings forth fruit in its season and its leaf also shall not wither and whatsoever he does shall prosper.

Joshua 1:8: *This book of the law shall not depart from your mouth but, you shall meditate on it day and night that thou may observe to do all that is written therein and then thou shall make thy way prosperous and thou shall have good success*

1Tim4:15-16: *Meditate upon these things; give thyself wholly to them; that thy profiting may appear to all.*

The principle of the word

Employ the unfailing power of the word of God. Decisions should be made according to the will of God. It is a permutation principle to locate the word of God and place your decision there. Base your decision-making on the sound word of God; the word of God should always be the standard for you as you make your decisions. Psalm 119:105: *Thy word is a lamp unto my feet and a light unto my path*

Principle of sound counsel

It is also an effective weapon that can help in decision-making. Have good mentors or counsellors who must be men and women filled with the Holy Spirit, packaged with wisdom and with specialist experience.

Do not make hasty decisions. You need to release and avoid tension that will remove from you the evil of unnecessary pressure that could cause you to make mistakes in decision-making. Take decision when you are well rested and not when you are feeling tired.

Be composed and stable. Bring yourself together; regain your sense of a well-balanced life. What you do in time of challenge is not to take decisions in haste. Challenges can make you disorganised, and therefore your decision should not be taken when you feel challenged.

Chapter Two

The Impact of Decisions

Whilst making the right decision can impact your life now and impact the generation next, the wrong choices you make can have a painful and lasting impact on you and the next generation.

Let us take a close look at some examples of people who made decisions that had serious impact on them and the people of their time. Even now, we can draw on their experiences and we are able to make or not make the kind of decisions that they made.

Wrong decisions could be the result of pride and ingratitude as observed with the case of King Nebuchadnezzar in the book of Daniel, who became an animal as a result of wrong decision he made. Furthermore, he lost his kingdom, lost his honour, lost his brightness, lost his excellence, lost his majesty and his value. However, when he realised himself, he was restored. Pride and ingratitude can cost you a lot of virtues while humility can restore to you what you may have lost because of pride. Life is run and managed by choice decisions.

Daniel 4:29: *At the end of twelve months, he walked in the palace of the kingdom of Babylon. The king spake and said is not this great Babylon that I have built for the house of the kingdom by the might of my power and for the honour of my majesty?*

While the word was in the King's mouth, there fell a voice from heaven saying, O king Nebuchadnezzar, to thee it is spoken; the kingdom is departed from thee. And they shall drive thee from men and thy dwelling shall be with the beasts of the field: they shall make thee to eat grass as oxen, and seven times shall pass over thee until thou know that the most high ruleth in the kingdom of men and giveth it to whomever he will.

Adam and Eve made a decision to eat the forbidden fruit and what was the result? They bought into Satan's rebellion and disobedience, thereby they lost their status and place with God. Adam's choice to disobey the word of God affected many generations, and even though Jesus Christ has come to restore man back to the position that God desired for him to be, it is only those who believe in the death, burial and resurrection of Jesus Christ that are restored. In effect, the wrong decision that Adam made, thousands of years ago, is still affecting the destiny of human beings until today!

Life is run and managed by choices. Whatever you are today is the result of the decisions that you made yesterday, and what you will become and where you will be tomorrow will be impacted by the decisions you make today.

You need to be determined to release the ability and the energy you require to reach your goal and overcome failure or fall and refuse to be down or discouraged.

Good decision will not only produce results for the present, but also for posterity. The impact of a good decision goes from one generation to another. Let us see a few examples:

Esther

Esther was a devout Jew who made up her mind to stand for what she believed in. She believed that God would grant her the favour that she needed to stand before the king, who was also her husband, without an invitation from him. Interestingly, she fasted and prayed before she presented herself before the king: she understood the importance of activating the power of God on her behalf and she did not act in the flesh. She backed her decision with prayers and today, many years after she made that choice, we still read about her and use her as a point of reference for a number of reasons, including her ability to make a wise decision, her determination to stand by such a decision, the boldness to go before the king without invitation. At that time, it was extremely unacceptable to appear before the king without invitation. Esther had the faith to expect the best in the face of strong opposition, and indeed death.

Jacob

In the book of Genesis 32: 24: *And Jacob was left alone; and there wrestled a man with him until the breaking of the day. And when he saw that he prevailed not against him, he touched the hollow of his thigh and the hollow of Jacob's thigh was strained as he wrestled with him. And he said, let me go for the day breaketh. And he said, I will not let you go except you bless me. And he said unto him, what is thy name? And he said, Jacob. And he said thy name shall be called no more Jacob but, Israel; for thou hast striven with God and with men and has prevailed. Jacob made a wonderful decision to wrestle with God and he got a reward; his identity was changed forever to Israel. Refuse to be casual, get up and get serious with God for the time is now.*

Abraham

Abraham made a veritable decision to obey God, he left the comfort of his homeland to a place where he did not know. As if that was not enough, God asked him to sacrifice his only son and Abraham agreed in faith! His reward was outstanding indeed as he is today the Father of Faith.

Leadership and Decision-Making

Your leadership experience is the product from your emancipated experience. When we mock people who may be struggling because we think we have arrived, we are teaching them to go and steal in order to arrive faster. They want to be rich now and they want to travel abroad because they believe that it is the best way to make it to the top: they want to become bishops and clergy. The result of this is that the churches begin to produce thieves, with false clothing of righteousness. When you lose the ability to fight, you will lose the integrity of climbing and the principle of process sanctioned by God.

The principle of valley experience is also teaching us leadership by process. Achievement by process involves; endurance, patience and long suffering, and it has the ability to stand any test of time.

A school of thought says that no one was born into this world already walking; no baby was born with teeth or talking. They get to it by process, which includes learning and observation. Experience is not invented, nor is it a mere mental story, but the reality of life experience in the journey of life. It is not what you jump over; it is what you pass through. What you pass through is what you walk over. Psalm 23:4: *yea though I walk through the valley of the shadow of death, I will fear no evil: for thou art with me thy rod and thy staff they comfort me.*

That which you pass through may be the pain of life that becomes your strength and power and your master testimony because you walk through it. You did not jump over it and as such, has turned out to be your wealth of experience. When you are talking, you can talk with confidence, passion and action without fear or intimidation.

What you are talking about is in you, not in the internet. An example is Jesus. He had an encounter with the word experience. He resisted satanic temptation; it took tough decision to do so and stay in God's divine perfect will through decision. He suffered and died for mankind and it was not an easy thing; he took tough decision to love and forgive those that hated him. When he died for all and rose from the dead, he rose for those that did not even believe. Romans 5:8 *but God demonstrated his love towards us in that while we were yet sinners, Christ died for us.* Jesus did not jump through the process of leadership, he walked through it. Even when he was offered to jump, he refused but rather preferred to walk through the process. His word was true and the reality of life, hence he said that his word is spirit and life.

It is not a magic, not a myth or a story, it is life and upgrade of other people's lives, and also the balance diet of the food for life. It is well cooked with experience.

Jesus as a master with a great price to be delivered for our well-being, says Isaiah 53:5-6: *but he was wounded for our transgression, he was bruised for our iniquities, the chastisement of our peace was upon him and with his stripes we are healed.* When the Bible says by the stripes of Jesus you are well, then you must realise that you are well, not that you will be well. He meant what he said and he said what he meant! The word of God is true.

Leadership is not about head knowledge or a crash course but the real-life practice. It is the concept of what you have passed through and your personal pain in the journey of life that has become your testimony to lead others.

Decisions set a new landmark in accessing new levels in your life. It is an instrument for a progressive plan that can cause you to take good flight for a new realm of life.

Sell into and buy into Principles of Decision-Making

When you allow other people to make decisions for you, or you accept the decisions that others have made for you, it is called 'borrowed decision' or 'transfer decision'. This kind of decision may lack organised values.

Decisions should not be made based on borrowed decisions as it usually tends to fail. Before you buy into someone's decision, make sure that you are very convinced about it and that you know it is what you are supposed to do at that time.

Decision is life and every life is run and managed by effective decision. Life should not be lived based on probability, trial and error or assumptions.

Decision-making is part of reality of life without which life is obstructed and does not go anywhere meaningful.

Real leaders are known by their ability to make and stand by good decisions without wavering. Any decision that makes you afraid is an error. It needs to be revisited for bold and effective decision.

Out of shoe leader

'Out of shoe leaders' are those leaders who are not able to make decisions, and many times it is because these leaders lack an administrative sense of decision-making. They are unstable, unreliable and therefore unable to stand by decisions. This can also be called a weak loss of power and authority of decision-making sense. The cure is to equip you by getting some skills. Improve on your abilities by way of studying.

Leaders who are not able to make effective decisions can set the house on fire without provision of a fire extinguisher because they function in failure.

Decision initiates focus, dedication, motivation, drive, hard work and commitment.

Decision breaks barriers, pulls down strongholds, runs the marriage and does many more. God decided to take care of man by sending his son Jesus Christ to die and today, anyone who accepts Jesus Christ as Lord and Saviour will automatically become God's responsibility. Decision is one of the most powerful weapons that are required to fulfil the race we run in this life.

Decisions should not be made based on imagination; it should be made with sound mind and judgement. It should be made based on true facts of life. However, every decision made by the believer should be backed up by the Holy Spirit.

Every important stage in life requires changes based on important well-balanced decisions you must make in order to enter your new and higher level.

Every fresh decision is a departure from the old and should enforce better values. You can work and move forward with decision power. Decision is the access for new levels; it gives the determination to insist and have advancements.

Determination gives the extra effort you need to make progress. The apostle Paul was determined to make progress in the midst of every crisis he had. Romans 8:35-39: *Who shall separate me from the love of Christ? Shall tribulation, or anguish, or persecution, or famine, or nakedness, or peril, or sword? Even as it is written, for thy sake we are killed all the daylong; we were accounted as sheep for the slaughter. Nay, in all these things we are more than conquerors through him that loved us. For I am persuaded that neither death, nor life, nor angels, nor principalities, nor things present, nor things to come, nor powers, nor height, nor depth, nor any other creature, shall be able to separate us from the love of God, which is in Christ Jesus our Lord.*

Paul decided to love God; his demonstration of trust in God was an act of the decision that he made. Decision-making helps our priorities and make bold men and women. God's decision for your life is a golden opportunity for you to make impact in your generation.

Every decision you make indicates your position with God. The power of making the right decisions really can never be explored completely. Life is run and managed by tough decisions. In Genesis 3:6, the Bible tells of how Adam and Eve made a deliberate decision to disobey the instruction that God had given to them: *And when the woman saw that the tree was good for food and that it was a delight to the eyes and that the tree was to be desired to make one wise, she took of the fruit thereof and did eat; and she gave also unto her husband with her, and he did eat.*

Their wrong decision to eat of the forbidden fruit 'brought them into the devil' rebellion and disobedience. Furthermore, the wrong decision that Adam and Eve made also affected the whole world. Cain decided to kill his brother Abel because, unlike his brother, he did not obey the Lord in that he did not offer his first fruit to God in the way that was required. However, his brother Abel offered to God a more excellent sacrifice. The difference between the performance of both Cain and Abel is their decision. Whatever decisions you make in life will determine the quality of life you will live in the end. Your choices are the deciding power of your ability to excel and reign in life. The decisions you make will determine if you will succeed or fail in the things that you carry out. Your decisions will either upgrade or downgrade your life. Abel was upgraded by his decision, even though he was killed by his brother Cain, whilst Cain was downgraded by his decision to kill his own brother, who offered a better sacrifice to God.

Adam and Eve failed in the midst of power and unlimited glory because they were distracted; they were engaged with the devil through friendly communication with him. *Evil communication corrupts good manners* says 1 Corinthians 15:33, whether you believe it or not. They bought into Satan's suggestion and made wrong decisions.

They were ignorant of their own glory and failed to protect the value of their relationship with God.

They had the problem of taking and obeying instructions, hence when the serpent asked Eve the question, "Did God say that you should not eat of this fruit?" Her answer was "Yes, God said we should not even touch it!"

They also had a major problem of indecision, and failure to make the right decision. They neglected their dominion power because Satan had no right whatsoever to question them, and therefore they were not obliged to answer him.

Whatever you neglect, you actually reject. They neglected the value of God's word, and they also failed because of a lack of self-identity.

They knew it not that they were masters, kings, boss over Satan, the image of God most high, and hence they still took instruction from their subordinate. This ultimately led to their downfall. Decisions, whether positive or negative, can affect generations.

The bad decision that was made by Adam was rectified by the good decision made by Jesus Christ. However, you ought to always remember that there may not always be room for another decision. It is therefore important to get it right the first time.

They failed to recognise the value of boundaries.

Life is protected and prevented from pitfalls due to recognition of boundaries. We are secure within boundaries and if we walk out of a set boundary, there are usually serious consequences. Adam and Eve walked out of the boundary set for them by God and they paid the price.

Daniel made a decision to not engage in anything that was opposed to his faith.

Indecision can initiate reproachful and disgraceful situation. When you do not decide on something, anything, the situation would usually decide for you and interestingly, when situations decide for you, it will not always be an honourable decision. Never let circumstances make your decisions because even though the decision may seem right at that instance, in the shortest of time, you will realise that such decisions will not stand trials or tests of time.

Indecision will also make you settle for less than the best, which will in turn affect your growth and development.

Indecision is a waste of time and possible resources. It wastes opportunity, can cause frustrations, affliction, disagreements and all manner of vices. It causes set back, obstruction, delayed productivity, and it is a killer.

Good decision:

- Eliminates distractions and gives you focus
- Helps you engage in specific assignments and vital priorities
- Establishes boundaries and operations
- Gives mental stability, overcomes worries and mental harassments
- Makes you well organised
- Creates peaceful atmosphere and comfort
- Facilitates actions, growth, development and expansion

Decision making and forgiveness

Forgiveness is a godly virtue and every believer has the ability to forgive. If you exhibit the attitude of forgiveness, you will be able to take the future by storm. There is no eternal future for anyone who will not forgive. Matthew 6:14: *For if ye forgive men their trespasses, your heavenly father will also forgive youth. And when you stand praying, forgive if ye have ought against any, that your father also which is in heaven may forgive your trespasses.*

Chapter Three

Vision and Visibility

Vision means: idea, dream, revelation and design. Visibility means to be noticeable.

Vision is working towards the purpose of God for your life. A life without vision is dead. Until you have a vision and you are working in that specific vision, your life is dead without purpose.

Vision is seeing and working towards your specific purpose. Knowing where you are going, knowing how to get there and knowing what to do when you get there. Vision flies on the eagle wings of purpose. We are strategically created to move forward.

God is very passionate about us making progress and moving forward with a sense of direction, hence he made us to back backwardness.

Our movement and drive in life is not a backward movement but a truest movement. We are created to work towards specific purposes.

A man with vision has a sense of direction and purpose, and can be likened to a person who is properly dressed for life and is very ready to walk to the top of his/her specific assignment. He is in a state of readiness and prepared mindset to score the goal of life. He has the ball, knows the goal post, has the right mindset ,which is to score the goal, and he is also in the right position to push the ball into the goal post.

Every goal scorer has the vision of winning and not to lose. Winning is what makes life meaningful, exciting and joyful. It gives hope and strength with more expectation.

It eliminates all fears, frustrations, confusion and distractions. Winning improves and increases expectation to win more. A person with the lack of vision is like a person who is naked and walking with his back instead of the front and has lost direction as well as that which he was wired for. You are not living until you have a vision and sense of direction.

If you do not know where you are going to, you go anywhere. People who do not know where they are going to end up following others to places where they may not want to go to.

What is visibility?

1. Degree of being able to be seen
2. The capability of being easily observed
3. The capability of providing a clear, unobstructed view
4. Clarity of vision or relative possibility of seeing
5. Degree of exposure to public notice

This is letting your light shine for your generation to see and buy into. Every vision should be on the eagle wings of visibility. It should be seated on top of the hill. Vision is for the people; it must be displayed for people to see it.

Matt 5: 14-16: *You are the light of the world. A city set on a hill cannot be hidden. Nor do they light a lamp and put it under a basket, but on a lamp stand, and it gives light to all who are in the house. Let your light so shine before men, that they may see your good works and glorify your father in heaven.*

1Peter 2:12: *Having your conduct honourable among the gentiles, that when they speak against you as evildoers, they may by your good works which they observe, glorify God in the day of visitation.*

Vision is commissioned to shine for the people to see so that they can run with it and buy into it. Every decision made should be clear enough for people to see.

Vision should be opened up for people to see. Habakuk 2: 2 says: *Write the vision, make it plain in tablets that he may run who reads it.'* Vision needs people, and people need vision. When people do not know the vision of an organisation, they become a liability instead of being an asset to the vision. Ignorance to the vision creates bondage.

Hidden vision has no future. Every vision that has future must be made known so that people can buy into it and run with it. Visions are not commissioned to hinder, rather they are commissioned to speak and provide services to the people. Vision is mandated to fly from the top level and shine down to the bottom so that people can catch it and run with it. It is not underground business, it is a top mission. The decision to make a vision known is the decision to communicate. In making the vision known, there must be effective communication because until the people know what the vision is all about, they will not be able to buy into it.

Deut 28: 1:1-13: *Now it shall come to pass, if you diligently obey the voice of the Lord your God, to observe carefully all his commandments which I command you today, that the Lord your God will set you high above all nations of the earth. And all these blessings shall come upon you and overtake you, because you obey the voice f the Lord your God.*

The Bible went on to list the different blessings that will come upon the one who obeys the voice of the Lord.

We are ordered as the head and not the tail, therefore our announcement must be from the top. Vision is the package of every leader, who has sense of direction and purpose for their life and generation.

Vision is commissioned to shine and that was why Jesus gave us the great commission. He commanded the disciples to go around and shine to the nations of the world through the preaching of the gospel.

John 1: 1-3: *In the beginning was the word, the word was with God and the word was God. He was in the beginning with God. All things were made through him and without him was not anything made that was made. In him was life and the life was the light of men. And the light shines in the darkness and the darkness did not comprehend it.*

Mark 16:20: *As they went forth preaching the gospel, God was with them and made them to shine more and more by confirming their words with signs following.*

Every vision must aim to have visibility for people to be attracted to it. Vision should be clear and readable. It must carry light, sense of direction, purpose, expectation, hope and delivery ability.

Vision can be made visible in different ways and through different means. For example, in the church, it can be done through soul winning and in non-Christian organisations or in the business organisation, it is called marketing. Believers are called to be marketers for Jesus Christ. The commission for soul winning was given by Jesus Christ himself when he said, "Go ye into all the world and preach the gospel." The proclamation of "Go ...Ye" was a mandate given to every Christian by Jesus Christ himself. Matt 28 19-20 says: *Go ye therefore and make disciples of all nations, baptising them in the name of the father and of the son and of the holy spirit, teaching them to observe all things that I have commanded you and lo, I am with you always even to the end of the age. Amen.*

The vision can also be made visible through the fruit of the spirit demonstrated by our character and our lifestyle. Our Christian lifestyle is a public Bible which can attract people to Christ. This should reveal the way we behave ourselves as light of the world.

Gal 5:22 says: *The fruit of the spirit is love, joy, peace, long suffering, kindness, goodness, faithfulness, meekness, temperance: against such there is no law.* The fruit of the spirit is the shining light of the believer. It helps to attract unbelievers to the kingdom. When you show divine love to people, when you shower others with goodness and when you release patience with purpose and you lend somebody a helping hand, it preaches in itself a full message and your mission statement that people cannot help but notice. People cannot reject love except when there is something wrong with their heads. Everybody wants to be loved and the fruit of the spirit is a very vital tool which we can use to express and make visible the life of God that we have.

Soul winning through the fruit of the spirit is a wonderful tool in reaching the unsaved. The Bible said: *by their fruit you shall know them.* The disciples of Jesus at Antioch were first called Christians because they behaved in the same way that Jesus did. Soul winning makes believers high class citizens and a star in heaven. Daniel 12:3 says: *They that be wise shall shine as the brightness of the firmament; and they that turn many to righteousness as the stars forever and ever.* Soul winning is a supernatural clothing required to be settled and seated in heaven.

Visibility of vision needs the following:

<u>Good advertisement:</u> For vision to be made known to the public. It needs to be advertised to create awareness; so that people can buy into it.

<u>Testimony:</u> Testimonies or witnessing is a powerful tool to make known a specific vision or the specific project. People like to identify with a dream or vision that has positive testimonies and references could be added value. By proclamation, which is also a powerful force to get the vision of the kingdom across to the unsaved world, we must go and tell them that Jesus Christ is Lord because they will not know except they are told. *For whosoever shall call upon the name of the Lord shall be saved. How then shall they call on him whom they have not believed? And how shall they believe in him of whom they have not heard? And how shall they hear without a preacher? And how shall they preach except they are sent? As it is written, how beautiful are the feet of them that bring good news.* (Romans 10: 13-15)

Power of invitation: This is one of the effective tools in reaching out to the unsaved by physically inviting them to Christ and his church. People respond to invitation: it is a powerful tool that works. God's supernatural intervention is through invitation. The call of salvation is by invitation. Jesus invited saying: *In the last day, that great day of the feast, Jesus stood and cried saying, 'If any man thirst, let him come unto me and drink. He that believeth on me as the scripture hath said, out of his belly shall flow rivers of living water'. John 7:37-41.* Power of invitation is a one-to-one tool of evangelism; it is a simple way believers can use to invite others to Christ and his church. The Samaritan woman at Jacob's well used this method and she emptied the city for Christ. She became the first evangelist in the bible (John 4: 28-30): *The woman then left her water pot and went her way into the city and said to the men, come, see a man which told me all things that ever I did: is not this the Christ? Then they went out of the city and came unto him.*

Outreaches and crusades are other strategies through which vision can be communicated and made visible to men.

Corporate Vision: the vision of the big house. Corporate vision is a shared vision that cannot be an island mentality or sole trader business. Vision needs people, and people need vision. For the visionary to be successful and make an impact, the vision must be shared. Corporate vision includes other people; they are invited to get involved because vision needs people. This is the example of Elisha's corporate vision of the big house.

The sons of the prophets saw the need for the big house. They took action, they bought into it and became a shared vision; they saw the need through the power of observation. They saw well. Jer. 1:11-12 says: *Moreover the word of the Lord came unto me, saying, Jeremiah, what seest thou? And I said, I see a rod of an almond tree. Then said the Lord unto me, thou hast well seen: for I watch over my word to perform it.* They took heed to the vision that means they made an investment of sort. This investment could have been time, prayers and finance in order to fulfil the vision. It was corporate investment for the furtherance of the vision.

For vision to meet and reach its goal and be successful, it needs multiple investments which could be physical, financial, material, mental or spiritual investment. Investing in the vision makes the vision run faster and also makes its delivery smooth. Making investment into a shared vision reveals a sense of ownership and commitment. People that invest in your vision or shared vision will likely feel your pain and share your values. People are unlikely to feel pain where they have not invested into and they are also not likely to pay attention to it because they lack s sense of ownership and value. When you invest into a company, and the company makes profit because you have invested and shared in their sense of ownership, you share in the profit. This also applies in the kingdom of God: where you have invested into the kingdom, you become a partaker of the share of the profit. 2Cor. 9:6-15 says: *but this I say, he that soweth sparingly shall reap also sparingly and he that soweth bountifully shall reap also bountifully. Just the same way that when you buy shares in a company, the dividends you get will be determined by the number of shares that you possess. When your vision is visible enough, people will be able to buy and indeed, they will reap whatever dividend there is to that your vision that they have bought.*

The sons of the prophets invested their lives, time and energy in the vision to further the organisational growth and possibilities. When you yield your life, time and energy into the vision of the kingdom of God, your life will never remain the same because you will reap the dividends of your investments. *God is not unrighteous to forget your work and labour of love, which ye have shewed toward his name, in that ye have ministered to the saints and do minister.* (Hebrews 6:10)

The sons of the prophets were determined through hard work with faith and prophetic evidence to ensure that they reach their goals and complete their mission. When one is determined then, there is the willpower and drive to fulfil a purpose.

The energy of determination comes with God's grace and the grace of God cannot be overemphasised because it is needed for a smooth flight into the arena of multiple successes.

Determination is one of the keys to success and promotion, therefore when there is lack of it there will be demotion.

The sons of prophets were committed to determination and hard work. Hard work does not kill; it only makes you happy and more fulfilled in the long run. *Seest thou a man diligent in his business? He shall stand before kings and not before mean men* (Proverbs 26:12). Hard work gives you better testimony and good standard of life. A lazy person has no future, *yet a little sleep, a little slumber, a little folding of the hands to sleep: So shall thy poverty come as a robber, and thy want as an armed man.* (Proverbs 6:10) But hard working people through grace and faith in God have a brighter future.

They respected leadership; they recognised and had the skills of following leadership. They needed guidance and direction and they asked Elisha to go with them in their new initiative for the advancement of their corporate organisation.

Corporate vision needs leadership with an understanding of corporate vision, hence the sons of the prophets refused to go alone without vision. Elisha was invited to lead the corporate vision.

Note that every corporate vision needs corporate leadership. Where there is no designated corporate leadership, someone usually rises up to take the lead and most times; it is done without even realising what is been done. No organisation succeeds where everyone is leading and no country in the world has two presidents or two prime ministers; it is always one and that one must be a leader that leads the entire nation. In every organisation, there must be a leader and followers: leaders are not followers and followers are not leaders. However, before you can be a good leader, you must have first been a good follower. The sons of the prophet recognised their level as the followers of Elisha, and Elisha was their leader.

Leaders are commissioned to lead and followers are commissioned to follow until they are trained enough to becomes leaders themselves.

The sons of the prophets understood the principle of teamwork. This is the spirit of working and pulling together toward the same direction where everybody aims to achieve the same objective. It is also where each of the team members contributes their skills and abilities to form a pool of resources that would initiate corporate success or team success.

Teamwork is one of the most effective and efficient principles that can lead organisations into outstanding testimonies and great successes. Members of the team take ownership of the vision because the people that have a sense of ownership in organisations invest their finances, time and energy into the organisation. They are determined for the organisation to succeed and make great impact in reaching their objectives and making outstanding celebratory success. Their overall desire for the organisation is for advancement and expansion. Not closing down but opening up and growing larger by the spirit of God. Ownership initiates commitment; it makes people be addicted to delivering and reaching their goals, in view of making achievements and multiple successes. Owners of things do not like to lose what they measure and possess. They will put all efforts to protect and retain it in order to make progress. They protect their organisation from shifting from its objectives through distraction and human errors.

They are willing to defend their organisation from internal and external attack without compromise because they are sharers of the vision.

They are able always to preserve the value and the image of the organisation without alteration, wavering or shifting from the vision.

Promote: The people that have sense of ownership promote the beauty of their organisation with the intention and desire to see people buying into it. They do not display themselves, but the organisational strength and beauty.

Celebration: People that have sense of ownership celebrate their organisation's success and value, and help to improve and develop work strategy in helping growth and advancement, for the good taste of the public and the advantage of the organisation.

Good testimonies when people in the organisation refuse to celebrate your organisation are your internal enemies: take note that it is not all people that are with you that are for you. Matthew13: 24–25 says: *The kingdom of heaven is likened unto a man which sowed good seed in his field but, while he slept, his enemy came and sowed tares among the wheat and went his way.* However, when you find such people in your midst, you should be able to make a firm decision to send them away at the right time. However, your first assumption should be that everyone is running with your vision. All members of the team must have the same identity, purpose and vision.

Teamwork helps to eliminate failure because everybody is expected to complement each other. It is a circle of expertise and specialise skills. It is also a circle of clear and positive influence. It encourages rich diversity that creates the right atmosphere which can make vision more noticeable, acceptable and accepted.

Romans 12: 4-7 says: *For even as we have many members in one body, and all the members have not the same office: so we, who are many, are one body in Christ, and severally members one of another. And having gifts differing according to the grace that was given to us, whether prophecy, let us prophesy according to the proportion of faith; or ministry; let us give ourselves to our ministry or he that teacheth, to his teaching.* The corporate vision requires such diversity and commitment in teamwork to make it visible and workable. Teamwork is a form of partnership that can bring in synergy and it is always better to work in teams. According to Ecclesiastes 4: 9-12: *Two are better than one because they have a good reward for their labour. For if they fall, the one will lift up his fellow: but woe to him that is alone when he falleth; for he hath not another to help him up. Again, if two lie together then they have heat; but how can one be warm alone? And if one prevails against him, two shall withstand him, and a threefold cord is not quickly broken.*

The Growth Mentality

The sons of the prophets envisioned growth and expansion. And they planned towards it. In everything that you imagine, necessary actions have to be put in place in order to fulfil the vision. This is what the sons of the prophet did. Their motive was an indication of their love and commitment to the vision of the big house.

They saw growth and possibilities, and they decided to run with it. Every environment has an atmosphere and if the people of that environment have good and positive thoughts, it inspires everyone to do the necessary things that can bring growth because growth is a product of positive thoughts. They envisioned growth, the worked for it and they got the result that they wanted.

The mindset of the team has to be the same, every member of the team must believe in the vision and in the strategies that are used to achieve the vision.

The bible said in Proverbs 23:7: *As a man thinketh in his heart so is he.* The words you speak are affected by your thoughts and the actions that you take. If you think rich, the likelihood is that you will become rich. You are the product of what you think. What you think is influenced by what you perceive with your senses. In order to think right as members of a team, you will need to think the vision of the team, be active in the strategies that are used to achieve the vision, and actively make it known to others in order to make it visible.

God works with thoughts and actions that is why God said in Jeremiah 29:11: *My thought towards you, are thoughts of good and not of evil.* This statement is a combination of sound thought and action

Vision and the power of thoughts

Until you think through, you cannot go through. The power of thought is very relevant in the pursuit of vision. The way you think will determine whether your vision will be achieved or whether it will die hopelessly. Thoughts empower and enforce the upliftment of vision. It is impossible to excel in the absence of well-balanced and excellent positive thoughts. That again means until you have thought through, you cannot go through. Ability to think through determines your ability to excel in your dream. Your creative ability is in your thoughts and imaginations. Whatever you can think about, you can actually achieve. Every thought and everything you can imagine can be achieved. A perfect example can be seen with the building of the tower of Babel in Genesis. Even God cannot stop the man that is full of imagination and can think through a course. That is why the enemy attacks many people's thoughts realm to deprive them from fruitful living and from making outstanding progress. It is only when your thought is fruitful that you can make progress. Failure of the mind will ultimately result in the failure of destiny.

A failed thought is the beginning of a failed person. My prayer for you is that your thoughts shall not fail, and that is why God instructed Philippians Christians to think right. Philippians 4:8: *Finally brethren, whatsoever things are true, whatsoever things are honest, whatsoever things are just, whatsoever things are pure, whatsoever things are lovely, whatsoever things are of good report; if there be any virtue, and if there be any praise, think on these things.*

The reason why many people are not making progress is because their thought realm has failed and has no light. The fuel of every winning positive thought is light. A mind or thought filled with light cannot be blind. It has overcome the obstacle of life and it cannot be deprived because he has a dominion power to access where he is going in pursuit of his goals.

You can lose or gain access to success through the direction of your thoughts; thoughts have power to direct people, thoughts can become a road map of influence, and that is why we must pay extra attention to our thought realm and allow it to be governed by the maker through the positive influence of the word of God and his holy spirit.

Thought failure; is the cause of any man's poverty. When you fail to think right, you start to lose. Your ability to think in life determines the extent to which you will go in making the right decisions and also making your vision visible.

The mountain of every man's confusion is the absence of positive thoughts, not thinking right and not thinking through. Ignorance puts you in bondage. Where there is ignorance, there is deceitfulness and untrustworthiness. The way to overcome ignorance is to make a powerful decision to get knowledge, wisdom and insight. They are powerful forces that have the ability to eliminate the ignorance of evil and bondage. Ignorance is the absence of light and knowledge is light: that is why the devil kept a lot of people from knowledge and information; many are deformed because they are not informed. When you are deformed, you are on house arrest with a restrictive order. To be deformed and not to be informed, is satanic strategy to keep people in fear and bondage, the same strategy Governments of the world are using.

The mystery of thought

Thought is a mystery that needs to be discovered and the good potential of it to be realised. It is loaded with ideals and creative information; until it is downloaded, you cannot be loaded with the benefits of the reality of life. We should pay attention to our own thoughts, as it is the hidden treasure of our wealth. Until our thoughts are liberated, we are not liberated.

When our thoughts are liberated from the bondage of traditions and restrictions that we have put on ourselves, freedom is not guaranteed and multiple successes cannot be sure. Life is governed by thoughts which are a product of what we receive through our senses, and the decisions we make are always influenced by our thought pattern. Your thoughts can create the wealth that you require on the earth, however you must train yourself to think the right things as admonished in Philippians 4:8.

Satan and his cohorts want to invest, spoil and to do their own will and the people of the world want it as well. Above all, God has given you the ability to access wealth and riches in the empire of your thoughts and when you get this wealth, he wants you to use it to his own glory. God wants the advancement of his kingdom and good will. Therefore, do not think devil and do not do devil, but think God and do God.

Climbing to the top of the agenda of God for you is important and not difficult at all. Luke 1:37, 45: *For with God nothing shall be impossible, for blessed is she that believeth for there shall be a performance of those things which were told her.* No one climbing the ladder of greatness thinks small. If you think you will not be able to get to the top or think that you will fall, surely you will not get there because you will definitely fall. The inability to direct your thoughts right will initiate your disappointment. Your thoughts attract to you whatever you think about.

Thought power is the power force of the drive of our pursuit in fulfilling our purpose. It is your thought that gets you to the top of the ladder before you get there physically. It is also your negative thoughts that put you on the floor before you get to the floor physically. We are not created for the floor but for the top. We have been made the head and not the tail. If we have no light in our thought, we will think confusedly, and distraction will be inevitable.

We can climb to the top of the mountain of outstanding success faster if we arm ourselves with divine insight, foresight, positive thought, winning confessions, faith, connection, and with supernatural light through the word of God. If you allow the word of God to fill your thoughts, you will be illuminated with divine energy and you can climb faster and get to the top without sweat.

Positive thought is the vital weapon in discovery and recovery; it helps to know where we are going and how to get there and what to do when we get there.

Constructive thoughts can help locate vital information that can initiate your victory. Arm yourself with valid and result-oriented information. Study to be informed and to show yourself approved. Lack of studies or information causes deformation and critical illness, and a high risk of bondage. Thoughts govern lives. The government of everyone's lives depend on our own thoughts. What you ponder upon can become what gives you direction. The Bible said as a man thinketh in his heart, so he is, you are what you think, whether good or evil. Thoughts are influenced by association, observation and teaching.

A man that hates studying and information hates life; he is likened to a man that is naked. Lack of knowledge is not promotion, but demotion. Foolishness is not elevation, but degradation.

In brief, you can conclude that thoughts are powerful and they influence you in the following ways:

Your thought determines and impacts on your direction, determines your behaviour, your actions, reactions and your responses, determines your weakness, your strengths and the way you handle your weakness. Determines communication, and also determines the art of communication. In addition, it determines your stability or instability as well as determines whether you will be focused on whatever you do or be distracted.

Chapter Four
Wisdom Keys

Your thoughts determine your drive and purpose. You should therefore make sure that you are equipped with the following wisdom keys

1. Wisdom is a divine gift from God
1 Corinthians 12:8: *That the God of our Lord Jesus Christ, the father of glory, may give unto you the spirit of wisdom and revelation in the knowledge of him.*

2. Wisdom is the key to life' treasure
Colossians 2:2-3: *That their hearts might be comforted, being knit together in love, and unto all riches of the full assurance of understanding, to the acknowledgement of the mystery of God, and of the father, and of Christ Jesus; in whom (Christ Jesus) are hid all the treasures of wisdom and knowledge.*

3. The fear of the Lord is where wisdom starts
Proverbs 9: 10: *The fear of the Lord is the beginning of wisdom: and the knowledge of the holy is understanding.*

Psalm 111:10: *The fear of the Lord is the beginning of wisdom: a good understanding have all they that do his commandments: his praise endureth forever.*

Job 28:28: *And unto man he said, behold, the fear of the Lord is wisdom and to depart from evil is understanding.*

4. The wisdom of man is foolishness to God and contradicts the wisdom of God

1 Corinthians 2:4-5, 12, 13: *And my speech and my preaching was not with enticing words of man' wisdom, but in the demonstration of the spirit and of power: That your faith should not stand in the wisdom of men but in the wisdom of God. Now we have received not the spirit of the world but the spirit which is of God; that we might know the things that are freely given to us of God. Which things also we speak, not in the words that man' wisdom teacheth, but which the Holy Ghost teacheth; comparing spiritual things with spiritual.*

I Corinthians 3:19: *For the wisdom of this world is foolishness with God. For it is written, he taketh the wise in their own craftiness.*

5. Relationship promotes or demotes

Proverbs 13:20: *He that walketh with wise men shall be wise but a companion of fools shall be destroyed*

1 Corinthians 15:33: *Be not deceived, evil communication corrupts good manners*

1 Timothy 6:5: *Perverse disputing of men of corrupt minds, and destitute of the truth supposing that gain is godliness, from such withdraw thyself.*

6. Wisdom of God is foolishness to the natural man

Proverbs 18:2: *A fool hath no delight in understanding, but that his heart may discover itself.*

Isaiah 55:8-9: *For my thoughts are not your thoughts neither are my ways your ways.*

7. Your communication reveals your wisdom

1 Kings 10:24: *And all the earth sought to Solomon to hear his wisdom which God hath put in his heart*

Proverbs 18:21: *Death and life are in the power of the tongue: and they that love it shall eat the fruit thereof*

James 3:2: *For in many things we offend all, if any man offends not in words the same is a perfect man and able also to bridle the whole body.*

8. Jesus is our divine wisdom

1 Corinthians 1:301 Corinthians 1:30: *But of him are ye in Christ Jesus who of God is made unto us wisdom, and righteousness and sanctification and redemption.*

Ephesians 1: 8: *Wherein he hath abounded toward us in all wisdom and prudence*

9. Wisdom of God promotes

2 Timothy 3:15: *and that from a child thou hast known the holy scriptures, which are able to make thee wise unto salvation through faith which is in Christ Jesus.*

Psalm 107:42

John 5:32

10. The treasure of wisdom are hidden in Christ

Colossians 2:2-3: *That their hearts might be comforted, being knit together in love, and unto all riches of the full assurance of understanding, to the acknowledgement of the mystery of God, and of the father, and of Christ Jesus; in whom (Christ Jesus) are hid all the treasures of wisdom and knowledge.*

11. The word of God is the source of wisdom

Psalm 119: 98-100: *Thou through commandments (word) hast made me wiser than mine enemies: for they are ever with me. I have more understanding than all my teachers: for thy testimonies are my meditations. I understand more than the ancients because I keep thy precepts.*

Proverbs 2:6: *For the Lord giveth wisdom: out of his mouth cometh knowledge and understanding.*

12. Wisdom is procured and secured by those who pursue it John 10:27 my sheep hear my voice and I know them and they follow me

James 1:5: *If any of you lack wisdom let him ask of God that giveth to all men liberally and upbraideth not and it shall be given him.*

Isaiah 40:31: *But they that wait upon the Lord shall renew their strength; they shall mount up with wings as eagles; they shall run and not be weary, they shall walk and not faint.*

13. The Holy Spirit is the spirit of wisdom that releases gifts, talents, potentials and skills

Exodus 31:1-4: *And the Lord spake unto Moses saying, See I have called by name Bazaleel the son of Uri, the son of Hur, of the tribe of Judah: and I have filled him with the spirit of God in wisdom, and in understanding and in knowledge and in all manner of workmanship. To devise cunning works to work in gold and in silver and in brass.*

Exodus 36:1: *Then worked Bazaleel and every wise hearted man, in whom the Lord put wisdom and understanding to know how to work all manner of work for the service of the sanctuary, according to all that the Lord had commanded.*

Daniel 1:4: *Children in whom was no blemish, but well favoured and skilful in all wisdom, and cunning in knowledge and understanding science, and such as have the ability in them to stand in the king' palace and whom they might teach the learning and the tongue of the Chaldeans.*

14. Wisdom births mercy. A believer that is well packaged with wisdom also has an attitude of mercy

James 3:17: *But the wisdom that is from above is first pure, then peaceful, gentle, and easy to be intreated, full of mercy and good fruits, without partiality and without hypocrisy.*

15. Wisdom is a powerful force which surpasses the weight of jewels and money

Proverbs 3:13-15: *Happy is the man that findeth wisdom and the man that getteth understanding for the merchandise of it is better than the merchandise of silver, and the gain thereof than fine gold. She is more precious than rubies and all the things thou canst desire are not to be compared unto her.*

Proverbs 8:11: *For wisdom is better than rubies and all the things that may be desired are not to be compared by it*

Proverbs 16:16: *How much better it is to get wisdom than gold! And to get understanding, rather to be chosen than silver.*

Job 28:18: *No mention shall be made of coral or of pearl for the price of wisdom is above rubies.*

16. Wisdom makes you wiser and more powerful than others

Ecclesiates 7:19: *Wisdom strengtheneth the wise more than ten mighty men which are in the city*

Daniel 1:17: *As for these four children, God gave them knowledge and skills in all learning and wisdom: and Daniel had understanding in all visions and dreams.*

17. The wise hates evil and evil hates the wise, they both operate in different directions. Just the same way light dispels darkness and the two cannot be in the same place.

Proverbs 1:22: *How long, ye simple ones will ye love simplicity? And the scorners delight in their scorning, and fools hate knowledge?*

Proverbs 9:8 *Reprove not a scorne*

18. Wisdom is a powerful force that is capable of revealing the hidden treasure, packaged within in.

Proverbs 19:8: *He that getteth wisdom loveth his own soul: he that keepth understanding shall find good*

Philemon 6: *That the communication of thy faith might become effectual by the acknowledging of every go0d thing which is in you in Christ Jesus.*

1 Peter 2: 9-10: *But ye are a chosen generation, a royal priesthood, a holy nation, a perculier people,: that you should show forth the praises of him who hath called you out of darkness into his marvellous light*

19. Wisdom carries the atmosphere of joy and peace

20. Wisdom creates an environment of joy by the spirit of God and peace that surpasses all understanding and human imagination

Proverbs 3:13: *Happy is the man that findeth wisdom and the man that getteth understanding.*

James 3:17: *But the wisdom that is from above is first pure, then peaceable, gentle and easy to be intreated, full of mercy and good fruits without partiality and without hypocrisy.*

21. Wisdom is a powerful weapon against the enemy

Luke 21:15: *For I will give you a mouth and wisdom which all your adversaries shall not be able to gainsay nor resist.*

Proverbs 16: 7: *When a man' ways please the Lord, he maketh even his enemies to be at peace with him*

Isaiah 54:17: *No weapon that is formed against thee shall prosper; and every tongue that shall rise against thee in judgement thou shall condemn. This is the heritage of the servants of the Lord for their righteousness is of me saith the Lord.*

Ecclesiates 7:12: *For wisdom is a defence and money is a defence. But the excellency of knowledge is that wisdom life to them that have it.*

Proverbs 2: 6: *For the Lord giveth wisdom out of his mouth cometh knowledge and understanding*

Proverbs 2: 12 *To deliver thee from the way of the evil man, from the man that speaketh forward things*

Proverbs 2:16: *To deliver thee from the strange woman even from the stranger which flattereth with her words*

22. Wisdom initiates supernatural favour which can be defined as unmerited favour

Proverbs 4: 8: *Exalt her and she shall promote thee; she shall bring thee to honour when thou dost embrace her.*

Proverbs 8: 34-35: *Blessed is the man that heareth me, watching daily at my gates, waiting at the posts of my door. For who so findeth me findeth life and shall obtain favour of the Lord*

Proverbs 3:1-4 *My son forget not my law; but let thine heart keep my commandments: for length of days and long life and peace shall they add to thee. Let not mercy and truth forsake thee: bind them about thy neck; write them upon the table of thine heart: so shall thou find favour and good understanding in the sight of God and man.*

23. Wise men and women don't mind been corrected. If you develop your skills in taking corrections, you will excel in life and also do excellent things.

24. Wisdom creates and increases wealth

Proverbs 8:18: *Riches and honour are with me; yea durable riches and righteousness*

Proverbs 8: 21 *That i may cause those that love me to inherit substance*

Proverbs 3:16: *Length of days is in her right hand; and in her left hand, riches and honour*

Psalm 112:1-3: *Praise ye the Lord. Blessed is the man that feareth the Lord that delighteth greatly in his commandments. His seed shall be mighty upon earth: the generation of the upright shall be blessed. Wealth and riches shall be in his house: and his righteousness undureth for ever.*

Proverbs 14: 24: *The crown of the wise is their riches: but the foolishness of fools is folly*

25. Wisdom can be impacted by the laying on of hands by Holy Spirit filled men of God

Deuteronomy 34: 9: *And Joshua the son of Nun was full of the spirit of wisdom; for Moses had laid his hands upon him and the children of Israel hearkened unto him and did as the Lord commanded Moses.*

2 Timothy 1: 6-14: *Wherefore i put thee in remembrance that thou stir up the gift of God which is in thee by the putting on of my hands.*

Acts 6:6-8: *Whom they set before the apostles and when they had prayed, they laid their hands on them. And the word of God increased and the number of the disciples multiplied in Jerusalem greatly and a great company of the priests were obedient to the faith.*

Acts 6:10: *And they were not able to resist the wisdom and the spirit by which he spake.*

26. Wisdom initiates promotion

Proverbs 8: 15: *By me kings reign and princes decree justice*

Ezra 7:25: *And thou Ezra, after the wisdom of thy God, that is in thine hand, set magistrates and judges, which may judge all the people that are beyond the river, all such as know the laws of thy God; and teach ye them that know them not.*

Proverbs 4:8-9: *Exalt her and she shall promote thee, she shall bring thee to honour when thou dost embrace her*

27. The words of the wise releases healing

Proverbs 12:18: *There is that speaketh like the piecing of a sword but the tongue of the wise is health*

Proverbs 15:2: *The tongue of the wise useth knowledge aright*

Proverbs 15:4: *A wholesome tongue is a tree of life but perverseness thereof is a breach in the spirit*

Proverbs 10:11: *The mouth of a righteous man is a well of life*

28. Wisdom is gotten through the principle of asking and receiving

Matthew 7:7: *Ask and you shall receive, seek and you shall find, knock and the door will be opened unto you*

James 1:5-6: *If any of you lack wisdom, let him ask of God that giveth to all men liberally and upbraideth not and it shall be given him.*

29. Soul winners are wise believers

Proverbs 11:30: *The fruit of the righteous is a tree of life and he that winneth soul is wise.*

Daniel 12:3: *And they that be wise shall shine like the brightness of the firmament: and they that turn many to righteousness as the stars forever and ever.*

Conclusion

The decisions you make are very important and therefore you must take enough time to consider them very carefully before making them. Every time you make a decision, you either make a positive or negative impact in your life and in the life of others. Decisions are life drivers, and a Christian should actively make choices based on the word of God and fully utilise the ability of the Holy Spirit that is made available.

www.ingramcontent.com/pod-product-compliance
Lightning Source LLC
Chambersburg PA
CBHW071033080526
44587CB00015B/2602